Love Poems

in Quarantine

Also by Sarah Ruhl

Love Poems in Quarantine

Sarah Ruhl

COPPER CANYON PRESS

PORT TOWNSEND, WASHINGTON

Cover art: Photograph by Sarah Ruhl

Copper Canyon Press is in residence at Fort Worden State Park in Port Townsend, Washington, under the auspices of Centrum. Centrum is a gathering place for artists and creative thinkers from around the world, students of all ages and backgrounds, and audiences seeking extraordinary cultural enrichment.

LIBRARY OF CONGRESS CATALOGING-IN-PUBLICATION DATA
Names: Ruhl, Sarah, 1974– author.
Title: Love poems in quarantine / Sarah Ruhl.
Description: Port Townsend, Washington : Copper Canyon Press, [2022] |
    Summary: "A collection of poems written by Sarah Ruhl"— Provided by
    publisher.
Identifiers: LCCN 2022004715 | ISBN 9781556596308 (paperback)
Subjects: LCGFT: Poetry.
Classification: LCC PS3618.U48 L68 2022 | DDC 811/.6—dc23/eng/20220203
LC record available at https://lccn.loc.gov/2022004715

98765432 FIRST PRINTING

COPPER CANYON PRESS
Post Office Box 271
Port Townsend, Washington 98368

www.coppercanyonpress.org

To Tony, William, Anna, and Hope—
all my patience, joy, and love
belong to you

Contents

Two. Poems written after May 25, the day George Floyd was murdered

Three. Haiku, tanka, and senryū in quarantine

EARLY SPRING

SUMMER

FALL

SPRING AGAIN

Love Poems
in Quarantine

One. Early days of quarantine

What are we folding when we are folding laundry in quarantine?

Standing four feet apart,
you take one edge of the sheet,
I take the other.

We walk toward one another,
creating order.

Like solemn campers folding a flag
in the early morning light.
But this is no flag.
This is where we love and sleep.

There was a time we forgot to do this—
to fold with and toward one another,
to make the edges clean together.

My grandmother might have said:

There is always more laundry to do—
and that is a blessing because it means
you did more living,
which means you get to do more cleaning.

We forgot for a while
that one large blanket
is too difficult for one chin to hold
and two hands to fold alone—

that there is more beauty
in the walking toward the fold,
and in the shared labor.

Easter poem during plague time (because there is no fake grass to put in your baskets this year, but there is real grass instead)

Don't paint the sky
it's already the right shade of blue.

Don't boil the sea into your broth
there is already the perfect amount of salt.

As for the grass . . .
put your feet in the dew.

There is not a thing you need to do
to sky, sea, or grass . . .

To the blue and the green of them
and the everything-in-between of them

in spring, when birds try to tell you the
untranslatable secrets in their song.

Menopause in quarantine

Oh second maidenhood,
at forty-six
my breasts are smaller,
for three months
no blood between my legs—
a new virginity.

My brain will be pregnant, not my body,
for the rest of this lifetime, at least.

*

Your birthday is coming and I must select a gift.

You tend to like things that are pretty because they are useful—
and so I buy you four mugs, and one knife holder.
We are almost out of mugs and there is no place to put the knives.

And I was correct—you loved your gifts.
Finally—a gift that is useful, you said.

The mugs are open for pouring,
the knives are ready to be sheathed.

*

Oh second maidenhood, second virginity,
is beauty use, and use beauty?

On homesickness, back when we traveled

What is your malady?

Asked the form at the community acupuncture clinic.
My pen hovered—so many to choose from:
the thyroid, the gut, the face.
I found myself writing:

Homesickness.

I handed in my form. I wondered if the doctor
with the needles would laugh at me,
but he said instead:

I am homesick, too.

And then he put needles in my ears and my ankles
and I fell asleep.
Around me, strangers slept
needled dreams, under warm blankets.

And I thought:
at home in the world.
The endless desire to be
at home in the world.

Behold and be-held

I want to behold
and be held by you

so close your features blur
do I see you rightly?
so far I can't quite touch your nose
do I see you rightly?

March

The fire goes up,
The snow goes down.
The ducks swim in their pond.

Your leg goes up,
My leg goes down.
Our bodies go round and round.

The sun in quarantine

My feet unaccustomed to grass
my eyes unaccustomed to sky

I try to be a sun for the three planets
who are my children

I borrow some of their warmth
in order to give it back to them

Regeneration

Consider the beauty of a horse.
Consider the beauty of a foot.

Then:

Consider a blister. From a burn.
How it covers the skin while it heals.

Consider its ugliness; or, how it
Hides the promise of new skin.

Then:

Consider the fact of considering.
Considerate children, considerate beasts.

And then:
How can one want to leave this earth?

Its horses, its feet, and its ugliness—
All of its terrible regeneration?

Poems and dreams are free

Poems are free
as dreams are free.

Dreams cost sleep,
and poems cost time;

we borrow night's lease,
and the currency of rhyme.

The bondage of money,
the bondage of time.

Unfolding on a crease,
dreams and poems stop time.

To Max Ritvo, who once said to me:

"I can't think of anything I could
disqualify as the spiritual centerpiece of a poem.
I don't think the spiritual world
needs to be claimed or reclaimed by anyone or anything.
Let religions lay hands upon it.
Let secularity lay hands upon it.
But let the hands be gently laid.
Let anything that clasps
offer the kind of prayer it wants to pray.
Let this all be poetry."

Let this all be poetry.

Today I wanted to tell you that this morning
my oldest daughter said she loves the sound of when
I write a poem.
What sound? I ask.
*The wood pencil scratching
against the paper,* she says.

I didn't know I made a sound when I wrote poems,
and that sound made me want to speak with you.

A spider in our bed

This morning I found a spider in our bed.
Last night you threw out my soup by mistake.
I was mad, and you said sorry.
Then I hurt your feelings about clearing plates.

At night I dreamed I bought my childhood house
for us to live in but it was wrecked, the ceilings caving in.
The lawn was occupied by a Tibetan furniture store.
I said they had to move out by Monday, and they said: *Tashi delek.*

Then the dog walked on her two legs holding two mice in each paw.
I told her to drop them.

This morning you made an omelet,
cracked eggs, stirred, applied heat,
fed the family, quiet.

We crack eggs and apply heat in a marriage,
hoping to make something that feeds us all.
We part eggshells, throw all that fragility in the garbage,
and hope not to break.

Then I took the spider in a jar and let it go
on the lawn.
What will that spider weave today?
Art, venom,
or an incandescent nest, temporary,

out of strong, tender thread—
and in the light, barely visible.

Differences between me and my dog

She poops in the road.
(Who says I don't?)
I poop in a bowl.

She eats from a bowl on the floor;
I eat from a bowl on the table.

She always bears small irritations with grace;
I sometimes bear small irritations with grace.

She likes to rub herself in the carcasses of dead animals.

Poems are good company

Poems are good company
when people disappoint;
people are good company
when poems disappoint.

Three kinds of light

for James

I have a friend named James
who loves the quality of light,
so he writes me postcards from Scandinavia
and describes the varied moods of light.
And today he wrote me that to his delight
there are in fact three kinds of twilight:

Civic, when you can do your business in the fading light—
your last bits of shopping, buy a button, deliver a plant,
see commerce fade.

The second, *nautical*—when you can still steer a boat and read a compass
before the stars appear—safe in the knowledge that day still guides your ship.

The last, *astronomical*—not actual night but a glow on the horizon—
that sliver you might call "effulgent" if you felt pedantic—
but the dictionary could barely define this not-quite-brightness—
a final breath of light before the day says goodnight.

And to conclude, James wrote that
the fact that there are three kinds of twilight—
means that what you think of as the night
is far shorter than you ever would have surmised.

In a year of plague, what seems eternal night—
we might be passing through instead
three kinds of twilight.

Finally he proclaimed, where he lives in England,
for an entire month in summer
there is no actual night.

When I saw this,
he wrote to me:
I cried.

Two. Poems written after May 25, the day George Floyd was murdered

White backup singers, June 1

I didn't want to watch that video,
but I did, I watched it. I watched a uniformed man
put his knee on another man's neck,
watched him press the life out, unmoved,
as though there weren't a man under the weight
of his uniformed body, as though the man under him
was a fly, or a dog.

I watched the Brown face lose life, minute by minute,
and I watched that white face, unmoved, impassive,
looking at some murderous internal horizon line.

From the privacy of my home I watched a man die.
And this whole country watched him die.
And this country came out of the privacy of their
homes and took to the streets.

And I hear my brothers and sisters saying:
white silence is white violence.
And I hear my brothers and sisters saying:
we are exhausted, can't you carry this burden for once?
And I also hear my brothers and sisters saying:
for one holy week, can you shut up, we are speaking.

And I say yes to both:
those calling for white people to speak up,
and those calling for white people to shut up.

And so a small offering, a middle way:
I will be your white backup singer.

Because I always hated the lyric in that Lou Reed song
about the Black backup singers who he asks to sing: Do do dee do do.
And then they do. Fuck that.
I will be your backup singer, if you want me to.
Even though I'm a bad singer.
I will practice. And I will stand behind you.

If Janelle Monae says say his name I will say his name: George Floyd.
And if Killer Mike says say his name I will say his name: George Floyd.
And if Alicia Garza says say his name I will say his name: George Floyd.

And if you tell me that you don't need me to sing
I will be quiet. And if you tell me I need to be louder I will be louder.
George Floyd. George Floyd. George Floyd. George Floyd.

Fire sermon

The Buddha said the world is
always burning.

What do you do when the world is burning?

Drink water, said one sage.
Light a match, said another.
Sit, said the original sage.

Stand, says a new sage.
She is fifteen, standing tall,
saying that she is a loud Black woman
and she is happy that she is loud,
and she will scream until she has no voice left,
and when she says:

Walk!—
we do.

Separating the laundry, June 6

I separate white laundry from colors.
I pour in bleach to make "my whites whiter."
Yesterday Breonna Taylor had her birthday
only she was dead.

And yesterday Donald Trump said *what a great
day it was for George Floyd*
only George Floyd was dead.

And I pour in a capful of bleach,
the same bleach Donald Trump advised
us to drink so we don't get the plague.
And I contemplate rage.

And think about my white skin while
I do my laundry.

Weekapaug

You walk down the street—
mostly white houses, mostly white folks,
and grey granite.
You are not white.
And you walk here every day.
We are strangers.
I wave. You wave back.

And the Central Park dog lady,
who I outwardly resemble,
hovers between us, a golem.

Inside my wave:
simple friendliness, or
do I want absolution
from my murderous race?

Inside your wave:
simple friendliness,
or the hope that I do not
enlist the state to kill you?

We walk on.
Every day we pass each other.
Every day we have the chance to love.

For Robyn Tamura

My friend left Brooklyn
for Connecticut
during plague time.

A white neighbor stopped by to
ask if Robyn's from China.

No, said her husband.
Japanese American.
The next day garbage

was dumped on their lawn. Cans of
baby corn, the offering.

When white neighbors move in, they
bake cookies, or bran muffins.

Whiteness near the Fourth of July 2020

1

I talk about whiteness on the phone with my mother.
I guess I'm so white I'm actually red white and blue, she says, laughing.
Red patches on my face, blue on my diabetic leg, some whiteness mixed in.

White is not a color.
Technically achromatic, a color without hue.
But if I were to paint my mother,
I would paint her red white and blue.

2

Don't cancel me,
she says.
Why would I ever cancel you, you're my mother,
I say.

She's seventy-six and alone during quarantine.
She's talking about how *Gone with the Wind* is racist with her film club
    on Zoom.
Talking about how Hattie McDaniel won an Oscar
but wasn't allowed to sit with the rest of the cast at the party,
so Clark Gable was going to boycott,
but Hattie McDaniel convinced him to come
and Hattie won her Oscar but they all sat at different tables.

My mother doesn't want to re-watch *Gone with the Wind*
and see it again with grown-up eyes.
She loved that movie as a child.

3

If you are mixing paint, it's useful to know that white is not a color and
black is not a color, they are what painters call shades,
wavelengths of light reflecting off objects.
No wonder white is so hard to see, so hard to paint.

4

When I was little, my mother used green makeup to hide her rosacea,
green and red are complementary colors; they cancel each other out.
I used to watch her cover her red skin in the mirror before she
went out to a party. She put on perfume, too.
She'd lost her sense of smell long ago when she hit her head on a tree.
So sometimes she would ask me to sniff her dirty laundry.

5

In places my skin is so white it's blue.
Crayola retired the crayon called Flesh in nineteen sixty-two,
the same year Martin Luther King Jr. was arrested for leading a prayer vigil.
Now that crayon is called peach and
Crayola offers apricot, black, burnt sienna, mahogany, sepia.

My skin is whiter than sepia, whiter than apricot.
The white crayon in Crayola doesn't work on white paper.

It's like spitting into water.
So most white kids when they draw their own faces don't color in the skin.
White crayon frustrates—
it doesn't show up.
White kids pretend our skin is the shade of paper and leave the outline
     alone.
I am the color of paper, thinks the white child without words,
so I am everywhere.

6

I am trying now to smell my own smell.
The smell of whiteness.
The way you don't think your own home
has a smell.
Everyone else can smell it, everyone else is like:
what's that smell?
but you're like:
what smell?

Do white people smell of old dead flowers pressed between
heavy musty white pages?
Do we smell of old blankets on which smallpox was
given as a present?
Do we smell of dirty laundry flung over the back of a chair?
Finally, do we smell like turtles? Putting our heads back in our
shells when we feel endangered, or walking slowly
away from history along the shore . . .

Prom, 1989

The only Black man
at my school stands with me;
I am so white my electric blue
dress reflects off my skin,
and we smile for a picture.
He's two heads taller than me.

My grandparents drive
from Iowa to Chicago for the occasion.
Before they meet my date in the kitchen,
my mother tells my grandmother privately,
"Just so you know, his father is Black."
A long pause.

Well, is he Black?
My grandmother asks.
I wonder if she's stupid or just hoping that my date
was an adopted white boy.
"Well, his father is Black and his mother is white,"
my mother says, "so . . ."

My grandparents are polite and friendly
to my date who is the handsomest man in Illinois.
My grandmother puts on her Midwestern charm,
and my date and I go off into the night.

We dance, I in my violently blue 1980s dress
with its terrible sparkles.
We don't kiss that night.
I'm still kind of in love with the
mathematician who dumped me
right before prom and then has the gall to ask me to slow-dance
to the song "Lady in Red," which I do.
I don't know if he dumped me because I wouldn't
have sex with him or
maybe his parents never approved—
he was Jewish and I was Catholic (see the part about no sex),
though I had long ago refused Communion.
I've always loved people who love outside of tribe,
color, caste, gender, God.

My grandparents ask me nothing about prom.
Later they ask my mother what came of it.
My mother says, "It didn't work out."
Good, my grandmother says.

*

Five years later, my father dead and my dog dying,
my former prom date appears in scrubs
at the veterinary hospital on Green Bay Road.
He appears in the doorframe,
holding my dying dog in a halo of light.
My dying dog is heavy and this man is strong.

I think he and I might walk somewhere celestial together,
where childhood dogs don't die
and dead grandparents are telling the truth
when they say they don't see color.

A white lady at a theater cocktail party

Is that your husband?
The dark one? The white lady points at the
only other man at the party who is not ivory.

He's my friend, not my husband, I tell her.
But your husband is dark, she says, clarifying.
I stare at her.

We all leave the party, my husband and my would-be husband,
and the two men laugh, each saying how handsome
the other man is—
it's a compliment, really.

And the theater party goes on, long into the night.

Fires

It is always morning somewhere on this earth,
and it is always evening somewhere else.

Of that you can be sure.
And somewhere it is burning.

As sure as the fact that, somewhere,
a brave person holds a little bucket,
trying to put out the fire.

The saving power of water,
the effort to put out the flame,

all our mornings and evenings,
all the things we cannot name.

Mothers' Day

Before the Hallmark cards are stuffed into their cases,
and before the roses are all sent out,
I read about the history of Mother's Day,
how the apostrophe mysteriously jumped
from Mothers' to Mother's, over time,
hiding the original purpose of the day.

When Mother's Day was Mothers' Day (meaning all mothers, plural),
Julia Ward Howe, an abolitionist and suffragist,
called for a day where mothers could work for peace.
When Mother's Day was Mothers' Day, she said:
mothers have had enough of their sons being murdered in wars—
we should love other women's sons as much as our own,
across nations, across tribes,
so that murder on a large scale never happens again.
When Mother's Day was Mothers' Day, she called upon women
to raise their voices, gather, sing, pray and insist upon peace.
She knew that peace was work.

Now that Mothers' Day is Mother's Day,
some women have breakfast in bed,
one day of appreciation for their labor.
Now that Mothers' Day is Mother's Day, we pay florists and
        stationery stores.
Sometimes mothers (I imagine them to be white) don't get a waffle in
        bed and are sad.

But the original Mothers' Day proclaimed:
Peace is as peace does.
To *make* peace, we say.
Peace is a doing, a making.

Can we get out of bed and do the work of peace?
To say: No mother's child should be murdered by the state.
And then to say out loud those mothers' names,
even as George Floyd cried out for his mother
before he was murdered:
Larcenia Floyd.
Tamika Palmer. Wanda Cooper-Jones. Gwen Carr.
Mamie Till-Mobley: who chose to keep her son's casket open
for all the world to see.

An end to apartheid in America

How and when will it come.
Birth can be violent.
Birth too gives way to blood.
Dangerous for the mother.
Dangerous for the baby.
Push too hard, you rupture.
Don't push at all, the baby dies.

How and when will it come?
And how much blood in the crowning;
how much blood on this country's hospital floor,
and who's gonna mop it all up?

Oh nurses, hold that mother's hand.
Her body's in a world of pain and
it's too late for an epidural—
plus the bystanders who want one
have been numb for way too long.

Babies come when they want to come.
And they cry when they take their first breath.

Three. Haiku, tanka, and senryū in quarantine

EARLY SPRING

Crossing

The water rushes—
and it doesn't stop rushing.
We help each other cross.

**Love poem to my husband, who
fixed the Scotch tape dispenser today**

The tape was unseen,
trapped in itself; you found the
beginning again.

Poppy anemone

What I did today:
saw the flower open in
daylight, then shut at night.

Was my poetry party a super-spreader?

There was a buffet.
Cheese platter, contagion, words.
Are my dear ones sick?

Haiku written with my son in March

The stores are empty
and the theaters are shuttered
but my mind is full

When in doubt, count

Count five, seven, five—
numbers for breath, word, silence.
Pink flowers open.

Nonessential workers

Wives or no wives, we
are now married to our houses,
and are we happy?

Yard

How long since you put
your bare feet on the soft earth
or on the hard stone?

Sleeping very late

I must need to rest.
Then rest from all that resting.
The new task, breath.

When I was a child I loved to watch soap
bubbles pop in the evening air

How many plans can
I give up with good grace? I'm
blowing bubbles—pop!

I lose socks in the
dryer. I buy more online.
The mystery of loss:

the more socks I get,
the more socks I lose.

Teaching on Zoom

In hand, a pen, in
mind, a pond; on-screen
fifty faces float.

For Kathleen

On hot flashes, she says:
do nothing—just remember
you're an animal.

Ambiguity of red

The black sparrow has
a red underwing: is it
for battle or love?

What day is it?

I keep track of the
days with my pill counter. But
sometimes I still

forget, when I go the wrong
direction, or skip Monday.

Koan

So much can be solved
with duct tape. So much cannot
be solved with duct tape.

Sisyphus

for John Lahr, who said:

Camus called the plague:
unbearable holiday.
I call it April.

For Elvis Costello, who said to me:

You know I love those
false near rhymes. A bent note on
a horn I can't play.

I will teach you how
to nap, but someone please teach
me how to wake up.

Quarantine, day 20

We are more and more
together, forced to gather
ourselves into time.

Look out your window:
it's interesting enough,
how wind blows the trees.

Dog mind

Dogs know everything:
love, hunger, grief; how to wait
for you to come home.

The woman who was bagging my groceries,
when I asked how she was, said:

*I can't sleep. They pay
more for unemployment than
for us to risk our lives.*

I hand her flowers. Behind
our masks, recognition, tears.

A riddle, the answer: live theater

You can't fast-forward
it and you can't take a crap
while watching it.

You must arrive on
time to it and yes—you must
be fully dressed.

Trio on Zoom

The three children play
violin out of time, but
with such hope that

it is beautiful.

I am running out of things to cook

Tater tots are the
food of the gods, but you can't
eat them every day.

For my oldest daughter

You start bleeding the
month I stop bleeding. The red
won't stop, life won't stop.

Now I measure time
with different stains, different sheets—
through her blood, not mine.

And that is enough for now

Day unfolded, the
children were fed three times, and
day folded back into night.

In the city I noticed
nothing but took in everything,
moon dwarfed by neon.

Swallow

Swallow sun, swallow
sky, swallow air. Follow the
diving swallows, there.

I read that people who groom more
during quarantine are happier and it seems
like a chicken-or-egg situation
but my friend tells me about foot masks
so I buy one

I peel and peel, and
a sudden softness under
all that hardness.

Time, which is measured by skin,
looks, in the garbage, like petals.

When will we ever
eat soup together again?
With real spoons, and steam.

**Midday, and the children come out
of their rooms where they have been
learning on screens**

Elsewhere, people rush.
I am content with my five
pretty bowls filled up.

Watching the food lines grow in
New Jersey

Starved for mercy, starved
for food. America
is starving.

How holy, that day
follows night. And how holy,
that night follows day.

It used to be very impolite

to cross the street
when you saw someone coming.
Now it is polite.

SUMMER

On a Zoom call, watching my in-laws throw my
father-in-law's ashes into the sea

Ashes, bones, marigolds.
My husband, children, a screen.
Open grief portal.

Remembering a time we could
eat oysters together

for Rachel

Oysters on a swaying
boat. A dog and baby sway
an afternoon away.

While I am on a work Zoom call, my son

came in holding a
purple vibrator, saying:
this won't stop buzzing

and it's in your sock drawer.
Can you turn it off?

**White people make bread while Black
and Brown people die in America**

We do not tend to
the sourdough starter. Mold,
green and grey, gathers.

What are we tending?
What are we not tending?

A negative test while the moon rises

Crescent moon, window.
You sleeping beside me, you.
I turned off the lights

in our room so I could turn
on the light of the moon.

Birthday haiku for Uncle Joe written on Zoom

Your son says:

A lot of people are just
waiting to die just so you
can eulogize them.

Love goes gentle and
in circles. So drive me home
to Mississippi Blvd.

You, with gentle eyes.
You, always with a speech and
a pat on the shoulder.

This summer

White people read *White
Fragility* on the beach
while Brown people die.

How white am I?

I am so white that
at family reunions
in Iowa we

wore matching Izods with our
names and corn on the lapels.

My daughter asked me when she was three:

Why does Dad have brown
skin and you have white skin and
why does Dad have brown eyes

and you have green eyes?
Is the answer genes? Or God?
Is the answer love?

On time zones

We ask Rich what the
future brings in Australia
tomorrow, where it's Monday.

He says, *I'm sorry to report,*
the future is no better.

My dog rubbed herself
on a bird carcass; the smell
of death protects her.

Still, we washed her clean twice.

Love and mess

Mess follows love and
love follows mess and both will
come trailing along . . .

Equal taste

Could I try to like
cycling uphill as much as
I like coasting down?

Coral

How to live outside
the skeleton, how to breathe
in water, how to

birth a jellyfish
without a proper father—
breathing outside of

skin and skeleton.
A dry brittle beauty born,
beauty that is dead.

How to live outside
yourself, in a tender film
of skin, waiting for

the crooning ship that
will one day do you in—how
to live in water.

Meditation, day 121 of quarantine

Blue, blue, green,
sky, water, and earth,
breath, mind, and body.

Polish the stone or the mind

The sand will scrub my
words away the sand will scrub
my skin away all

that is left is water

Walking in the dark

Eyes grow accustomed
to night the way the heart grows
accustomed to light

In Tibet it is said that when

the sunlight comes in
from outdoors, touching the wood
on your floor: it is holy.

Watching the bird fly standing still

A bird soaring looks
much like a bird standing still.
So, too, the mind.

Shelter

To love a house not
because it's perfect but because
it shelters you

To love a body
not because it's perfect but
because it shelters you

Move your pants before the tide comes in

For people who live
by the sea, the tide goes out;
metaphor, taking

shoes and lives with it. How fast
the tide goes out
how fast it will come in.

Time decides

for Michelle M., who said:

Scabs do not always
turn into scars.
Time decides, grace
and skin fold in.

For Anne's seventy-sixth birthday

Picking blueberries
waist-high in water, unmasked.
Cold water, sweet taste.

Sunset

And every day we
get to practice going to
sleep and waking up.

For Tony

Time has a way of
falling on top of me, big.
You make time smaller

so we can work and play inside
it better: morning, and afternoon.

And today all that happened was

my dog got hiccups,
so another dog licked her
eyeballs until her

hiccups went away. The
gestures of love between dogs.

Communion wafer in the night sky

How can the moon hold
you, when it can't hold itself—
dangling in the sky?

For Anne

There's God, you said, and
pointed at the light on the
water. We all looked.

Night-blooming cereus

for Paula and Anne

They bloom once a year
overnight. So we take turns
putting our noses

into white petals—
they seem to say: we opened
for you, do you see?

On entitled Brooklyn parents

I think: *those people*—
and then correct myself and
think: oh, oh! People.

For John Cage, who said:

*Begin again. Get
out of the cage you find
yourself in.* Funny

that his name is Cage.

My dog tries to walk into our old house

My dog tries to walk
back into the past, as if
the past were a smell.

The past is present
only in the nose: oh holy nose.
How the dog strains against the leash.

Lawn mowers and Bashō's grass pillow

Lawns too manicured—
too stiff, too green, too noisy.
Give me wild grass and sky!

You ask me to look in your eyes, and the familiar and unfamiliar rhyme

I see our history—
always, and still, the mystery
of what you carry.

If a dead butterfly can still fly,
what does that signify?

A yellow butterfly
came to us dead. I try to
sweep her up. Her wings,

separated now in three,
still move in the air.

Can sea cucumbers be instructive?

Time hasn't happened—
it *is happening*—the way,
says my daughter, a

sea cucumber breathes out of
its own anus: breath and waste.

My children are baking bread again

for Yangzom

And somewhere else, a
heart almost stopped. A woman
praying with her beads.

It was not a day for singing

It was a day for
feeding myself soup and for
eating-alone quiet

Large waves and children

Another wave! I
say idiotically, as
though they'll ever stop.

Immortality through property

We think if we buy
property we might live as
long as the house lives.

But our bodies are rentals;
our hearts not made of stone.

On a walk I saw a snake, a rabbit, and a dead rat

The dead rat: ego.
The snake's continuous
movement killed the rat.

But the rabbit said:
keep moving; continue in joy.

**I am a messy cook and this annoys
my husband who is an orderly cook**

The food and dishes
fly out of reach like planets
out of orbit and

I can't put them back in place
until after I've eaten.

**I think about patience while I
chop mushrooms**

Why is it easier
to wait for things you *make* than
to wait for what is bought?

My hunger stills as
I chop. And I eat the smell of
mushrooms sizzling in the pan.

To my children

Stand sturdy against
the waves or else let them take
you gently to shore.

This morning

Kiss you here, kiss you
there. I, a singing fish, and
you, my husband.

Today

The marigolds a
stranger gave us yesterday
are wilted and tired today

What is a child's duty?

I want to see my
mother but seeing her could
endanger her life

Quarantine in August, the overripe month

I'm tired of summer.
I crave fall. Luckily fall
comes after summer.

And if I get tired of it all,
winter will come, then spring.

FALL

Cause and effect

Does the wind move the trees,
or do the trees move the wind? A
child might ask, or God.

Meditation, day 207

What is filling me?
Nothing. What is filling me?
Everything. Soup, sky.

Your body, a temple

Your body, a temple;
I enter, and duck. Light pours in;
rain, through the rafters.

Attempt at holding opposing
truths in the mind

Nothing matters. Or:
everything matters? The sun
on my daughter's face.

Don't store your anger,
acorns for the winter frost.
Roll away, roll away.

A photo from when I was sick

I was skinny like
a woman in a painting.
Now I'm fatter like

a woman in her life.

Waiting for a storm

Rain threatens. We watch
and wait. The green tree under
the storm cloud, impassive.

A shuttered business

The sadness of an old
sign with painted-over letters—
"Benny's" showing through.

There is no cure for
yearning. Even the trees bend
in the wind like that.

Bell's palsy, ten years out

A crooked smile is
better than a crooked heart;
open me to God.

Could I live in the
color of my teacup for
a little while?

Books as food

Change the body by
what you fill it with; and so
too the mind—with books.

Tomorrow and tomorrow and time zones

And if it's always
tomorrow elsewhere and if
it's yesterday here,

then what is a day in time?
What is a day out of time?

An argument

When you're cold to me
the sun itself is not warm,
my skin is clammy.

I wear your sweater for extra warmth

The bite of fall air.
Your sweater is warm, big, the
almost-feel of your arms . . .

Is God a who or a what when the world falls apart?

Who is the God who
does such things? *Who* is the wrong
word, but *what* is the God

sounds wrong, too. Oh pronouns.
Oh, sad unknown grammar.

Do you have grief to spare?
Then who will you spare it on?
A friend or a stranger?

Books don't spread germs

The libraries may
be closed for now. But the
books are wide open.

Block Island

Searching for glass orbs,
all we found was garbage. But,
the sea, oh the sea!

Election day is windy in Rhode Island
and the weather report says that

mariners should seek
safe harbor, alter course, or
remain in port.

I thought it was mist . . .
but it was laundry steam.
Still mystical to

make dirty clean.

Alchemy

Stop trying to make
things out of things and instead
love the core, the fruit.

I was a child of
pavement then. My new life has
frost on the grass.

Hungry ghosts

I am hungry and
so: I am hungrier. I
can't stop my hunger.

WINTER

As the days get shorter and shorter

You can see the light
inside the darkness, but the
reverse is not true.

Today I learned that in kindergarten, a
boy named

Cosmo Music told
Hope there was no Santa Claus.

But his name is Cosmo Music?
Surely there is a God.

My first love came with
the first snow. Both melted.
Snow comes every year.

Snowstorm

There are moments I
forget to breathe and moments
when I remember.

Again, snow

The clarity of snow
in an empty field makes me
believe again in

an empty piece of paper

Still life

A lightbulb, a cup
of coffee, Scotch tape. What sticks,
what enlivens: WAKE!

When I see you again

There will be lightbulbs—
and there will be lightbulbs—
or no light at all.

Computers can be
dreadful for writers—on paper
you can't buy a thing.

The moon rises just
as surely over an ugly
house as a pretty one.

Just as a dog shits on
any old kind of lawn.

**I made two false assumptions
looking at a red cardinal**

One—the bird was not
trying to get in the car.
She was looking in

the side mirror. Two: *she* was
really a *he*—vain bird.

Tanka, January 6

Forced entry—a door—
a hall—a mouth—a land—
a man in horns and

furs inside, his rage complete.
Our sorrow still incomplete.

Boiling water isn't mad at the tea

You can say you're mad
at me. I won't break and we
won't break. Tea still poured.

This field. This snow. This
stone. This this this—what I did
not know I loved.

Are you studying
every day how to love
or how to die?

It is warm enough today
for a foot in the long grass.

Meditating outdoors

I look at a hole
in a stone wall. I move. Now
I can't see the hole.

Seeing must have something
to do with where I sit.

Playing card games with others

shows that you value
people more than time—which is
time well spent.

But I still hate cards.
And like people.

Meditation, January 18

Without faith, still you
can practice. Without practice
or faith—Doritos.

Meditation, January 19

My comparing mind
smells like a bad fart—
a rat's hard-boiled egg.

Nap

Rest in the light a
little longer. Sleep may come
or go. The dog stays.

Late afternoon

The smell of rice as
it boils, the color of moss,
people listening.

Lesson from quarantine

If you don't have a
lock on your door, make love
up against it, standing.

Upon waking

I place my foot on
your foot. It fits there. And so
our feet remain, paired.

Winter in Illinois

My mom tied my scarf
around my face. Warmth, the smell
of wool—her warm hands.

A person can be pedantic about anything

Tax code, the spirit,
art, wood, math, and even love.
Hearts don't talk in words.

Counting the stars is impossible

Eternity is
scary when you live inside
time all the time. Count

the days with things beyond
measure; the stars will resist.

I'm scared of the desk today, so

don't write at the desk.
It's boring, and made for work.
A field will hold me.

The doors don't quite shut
in this house that is not ours:
so, keep the doors open!

And I was so happy

teaching my son to
roll up a pair of socks
on this clear morning

Why is my gaze so
low? All those stone walls . . . the trees
yell: look up at me!

Passage from one yard to another

Today, after weeks
of looking, I saw that the
stone wall has another

hole in it, another way
to get through . . .

And all the frozen snow melted today

The melting and the
freezing; the shape of a year,
the shape of a heart.

I don't know anything about time

But I know that the
spring birds are thinking about
coming home again.

SPRING AGAIN

And after all that

why not worship the
sun? When it's light again at
dinnertime—oh sun.

A year since quarantine began

Time stopped and time will
begin again. May our
measures change, soften.

I am lucky: when
I smell fresh, cold air I think
of being a child.

What of my eyes and their infallibility?

The horizon looks
like a line, but the world is
a circle so . . . huh.

I no longer know
how long a day is—enough
time to find a lost poem?

There are things I must
do but not today. I am
too busy sitting.

Instead of writing,
I should water my
dry plant.

My glasses sit on the rug

Glasses without a
face; books without a reader:
cup without water.

Scrolling upon waking up

Do I need a view
into the lives of others
to wake up to life?

I have brought my dog with me. Why?

for Jorge

Because everything
in life is better with a
dog. Except for sex.

What is the holy name, you or the Lord?

For some it is the
blue bottles lining their walls.
For others, it's God.

After the long winter

A window—and I
open it. The wind smells of
warm grass and sunlight.

My dog writes for me
while she dreams. I, awake, take
dictation, drink tea.

Freedom

I will interrupt
my own mind. Instead of others
interrupting me.

Horse racing

Do horses know they
are racing each other or
are they just running?

The volunteers at the senior center
vaccine parking lot,

Doreen and Beryl,
volunteered to save our lives.
Could there be goodness?

Six months without a barber and

your hair is a field
of wild grass going this way
and that in my hands

Equinox

My heavy jacket's
zipper is broken. Oh well.
Sunlight warming me.

Seeing or showing

You can see my face—
but will I *show* you my face?
Lift my hair and eyes?

Noon

The things I know I
have known and will know again:
your face, that field, sky.

After all, it is irrational to be afraid of
mold, which will come unless you eat
the fruit

I don't want to fear
the life cycle anymore:
death, mold, and endings.

It is absurd to fear the
blue mold on a tomato.

Walking in a spring rain

Sometimes bullies feel
like the weather—but they
are not the weather.

As in chess and other games

if a pawn does not
leave the game she can become
one of many queens.

For three years I

opened the door to
monsters and they walked in and
asked for water

Sometimes God is when strangers touch

And we've been without
touch for so long. I pay cash
for dog food and my

hand touches the storekeeper's hand.
Goodbye, friend, he says as I leave.

Needs

A secret singing
voice needs so much dark quiet
and not much money.

Changing the locks

When you change the locks,
gold dust falls on the lintel:
who's in, who's out?

When my daughter heard the story of Oedipus

she thought it should be
a comedy instead of
a tragedy.

My dog sits zazen
much longer than I can. Moo!
Then she drinks water.

I will try to

sit at the dinner
table a little longer
to laugh and not clean

There is a house somewhere

The house has winter
in the backyard, summer in
the front yard, and birds . . .

**I read somewhere that your cuts heal
faster when you are in love and today**

I fell backward into
a flowerpot. You cleaned my cut
the way a mother would.

I want to be a
student again, looking at
rain on a glass roof.

Morning dove

I used to spell that
bird *morning* dove. Until I
listened—oh, *mourning*!

Talking things over, we looked up and saw

two wild geese tamed by—
what?—love?—sticking their two long
necks into one future.

I, on top of you, looking at your face, and

I said: *how did God*
make you so beautiful and
you said: *to please you*

In the place where you were born

The ground might feel more
like ground. The trees might feel more
like trees. Why then leave?

You can't come home if
you never leave. Behind that
tree is another tree.

Another storm

Big storm, trees felled, now
roots tilt up not down. Yellow
trucks clean up debris.

The window is shut
but my heart is open. And
so the wait begins.

**I learned that quarantine meant 40 days
and now it's day 400**

Then the sun came out
after five days of rain. And
there was so much green.

What the earth does well:
beauty as evidence of
change: leaf, sap, flower.

Poem catching

I catch the poems in
the morning, half-asleep. Then
day comes, and dishes.

Where is the birdcall?
In the air, in your chest? Or
there—where the song is.

My mother, who loves etymologies, told me that *quarantine* comes originally from the Italian term *quaranta giorni*—meaning "forty days": forty days for ships to sit in ports so they would not infect the city. I thought when I reached forty haiku (and tanka, a variation on haiku) I could suspend my quarantine practice. And yet this cessation of activity will last much longer than forty days. And so I kept going.

Forty days in the desert, forty days and nights of rain for Noah, forty days for a woman to rest after childbirth. How many days will it take for this country to remake itself? Will this country remake itself?

I stand before you in a great deal of uncertainty, writing what comes, as a practice.

*

Most of these love poems are for my husband, Tony. He happens to be biracial, half Thai, what you might call *hapa,* depending on your preference. My kids are a quarter Asian though they look white. And does that mean that all my love poems to my husband are saturated in the meaning of our different skin tones? Or are some love poems simply love poems?

I stand with Jericho Brown, who writes, "I begin with love, hoping to end there." How can we broaden our love, love strangers as much as we love our intimates? To write love poems to our very particular beloveds, and also write love poems to the world and its many tribes.

bell hooks writes, "I feel our nation's turning away from love . . . . Turning away we risk moving into a wilderness of spirit so intense we may never find our way home again. I write of love to bear witness . . . and to call for a return to love."

Love animates the word. Love animates the world. I humbly stand before the blank page, hoping to see you there.

Acknowledgments

Paula Vogel and Anne Sterling for shelter during the pandemic, where many of these poems were written. The New York Zen Center for Contemplative Care for ninety days of meditation. William Duprey for more meditation. The Pickle Council for reading all the poems in progress: Keith Reddin, Andy Bragen, Kathleen Tolan, Lily Thorne. Other early readers: Ellen McLaughlin, Erin Crowley, Jessica Thebus, Kathy Chalfant, P. Carl, Michelle Memran, Melissa Crespo, Robyn Tamura, Sherry Mason, Mark Epstein, Emma Feiwel, Dorian Karchmar. Much gratitude to Michael Wiegers and John Pierce. Thanks to Lauren Cerand. Thanks to many of the dedicatees in the poems, including James Platt, Max Ritvo, Rachel Weisz, Elvis Costello, John Lahr, and my dog Minerva, who I guess will never read these acknowledgments. And most of all, to Tony, William, Anna, and Hope—all my patience, joy, and love belong to you.

About the Author

Sarah Ruhl is a playwright, essayist, and poet. She is a MacArthur Fellow, two-time Pulitzer Prize finalist, and a Tony Award nominee. Her book of essays, *100 Essays I Don't Have Time to Write,* was published by FSG and named a Notable Book by the *New York Times.* Her book *Letters from Max,* coauthored with Max Ritvo and published by Milkweed Editions, was on the *New Yorker*'s Best Poetry of the Year list. Her plays include *For Peter Pan on Her 70th Birthday; How to Transcend a Happy Marriage; The Oldest Boy; Stage Kiss; Dear Elizabeth; In the Next Room, or the Vibrator Play; The Clean House; Passion Play; Dead Man's Cell Phone; Melancholy Play; Eurydice; Orlando; Late, a Cowboy Song,* a translation of Chekhov's *Three Sisters,* and others. Ms. Ruhl's plays have been produced on and off Broadway, around the country, and internationally, where they've been translated into more than fifteen languages. Originally from Chicago, Sarah Ruhl received her MFA from Brown University, where she studied with Paula Vogel. She has received the Susan Smith Blackburn Prize, the Whiting Award, the Lilly Award, a PEN award for midcareer playwrights, the National Theatre Conference's Person of the Year Award, and the Steinberg Distinguished Playwright Award. She teaches at the Yale School of Drama and lives in Brooklyn with her family.

Poetry is vital to language and living. Since 1972, Copper Canyon Press has published extraordinary poetry from around the world to engage the imaginations and intellects of readers, writers, booksellers, librarians, teachers, students, and donors.

COPPER CANYON PRESS WISHES TO EXTEND A SPECIAL THANKS TO THE FOLLOWING SUPPORTERS WHO PROVIDED FUNDING DURING THE COVID-19 PANDEMIC:

4Culture
Academy of American Poets (Literary Relief Fund)
City of Seattle Office of Arts & Culture
Community of Literary Magazines and Presses (Literary Relief Fund)
Economic Development Council of Jefferson County
National Book Foundation (Literary Relief Fund)
Poetry Foundation
U.S. Department of the Treasury Payroll Protection Program

WE ARE GRATEFUL FOR THE MAJOR SUPPORT

PROVIDED BY:

TO LEARN MORE ABOUT UNDERWRITING
COPPER CANYON PRESS TITLES,
PLEASE CALL 360-385-4925 EXT. 103

WE ARE GRATEFUL FOR THE MAJOR SUPPORT
PROVIDED BY:

Richard Andrews
Anonymous (3)
Jill Baker and Jeffrey Bishop
Anne and Geoffrey Barker
In honor of Ida Bauer, Betsy
  Gifford, and Beverly Sachar
Donna Bellew
Matthew Bellew
Sarah Bird
Will Blythe
John Branch
Diana Broze
John R. Cahill
Sarah Cavanaugh
Stephanie Ellis-Smith and
  Douglas Smith
Austin Evans
Saramel Evans
Mimi Gardner Gates
Gull Industries Inc. on behalf of
  William True
The Trust of Warren A. Gummow
William R. Hearst III
Carolyn and Robert Hedin
David and Jane Hibbard
Bruce Kahn
Phil Kovacevich and Eric Wechsler

Lakeside Industries Inc. on behalf
  of Jeanne Marie Lee
Maureen Lee and Mark Busto
Peter Lewis and Johnna Turiano
Ellie Mathews and Carl Youngmann
  as The North Press
Larry Mawby and Lois Bahle
Hank and Liesel Meijer
Jack Nicholson
Gregg Orr
Petunia Charitable Fund and
  adviser Elizabeth Hebert
Suzanne Rapp and Mark Hamilton
Adam and Lynn Rauch
Emily and Dan Raymond
Joseph C. Roberts
Jill and Bill Ruckelshaus
Cynthia Sears
Kim and Jeff Seely
Joan F. Woods
Barbara and Charles Wright
In honor of C.D. Wright,
  from Forrest Gander
Caleb Young as C. Young Creative
The dedicated interns and
  faithful volunteers of
  Copper Canyon Press

The Chinese character for poetry is made up of two parts:
"word" and "temple." It also serves as pressmark for
Copper Canyon Press.

The poems are set in Garamond Premier Pro.
Book design and composition by Phil Kovacevich.